M000207508

A City Vision All Leaders Must Have

*Cultivating a Passion
to Impact Your City*

LIFE IMPACT SERIES

FRANK DAMAZIO

CityChristianPublishing

www.CityChristianPublishing.com

PUBLISHED BY CITY CHRISTIAN PUBLISHING
9200 NE Fremont, Portland, Oregon 97220

City Christian Publishing is a ministry of City Bible Church and is
dedicated to serving the local church and its leaders through the
production and distribution of quality equipping resources. It is our
prayer that these materials, proven in the context of the local church,
will equip leaders in exalting the Lord and extending His kingdom.

For a free catalog of additional resources from City Christian
Publishing, please call 1-800-777-6057 or visit our web site at www.
CityChristianPublishing.com.

A City Vision All Leaders Must Have

ISBN: 1-59383-034-3

First Edition, July 2006
Printed in the United States of America

CONTENTS

Part 1: A Vision for Your City......................................7
If God has called you to your church, he has called you to your city. A relationship with a city is similar to a romance, with a mixture of love and pain, joy and sorrow, pleasure and disappointment, glory and gory days. The challenge is to understand the vision for your city and work God's plan to make that vision a reality.

Part 2: Keys to the City...35
God gives to churches the keys to open cities that have been locked and declared off-limits by the enemy. Church leaders must unite with a single vision to glorify God and establish God's kingdom throughout their chosen cities.

**Part 3: Securing Borders
and Reclaiming our Cities**..59
Many cities are filled with violence, drugs, gangs, prostitution, and poverty. But this is not God's intention for these cities. Church leaders must claim cities for God through a spiritual invasion based on biblical promises and the power of intercessory prayer and repentance.

Part 4: Leading Cities into the Light......................111

Many Christian leaders have been content to remain in the comfort zone, rescuing those who manage to find their way to church doors. But now it is time to march into the depths to free those who are locked in darkness and bring them into God's light.

Part 1:

A Vision for Your City

*Thus says the Lord God: "On the day that
I cleanse you from all your iniquities, I will
also enable you to dwell in the cities, and the
ruins shall be rebuilt."—Ezekiel 36:33*

My relationship with my city is in many ways like the relationship I have with my wife; it's constantly growing. I loved her when we got married, but the more I know about her hidden personality, her unique gifts, and her stalwart character, the more I love her. My love grows as our relationship grows and we experience more of life together: home, children, sorrow, pain, joy, disappointment, challenges, and surprises.

When a pastor is called to a city, the bonding process is uniquely parallel to a romance, a marriage, a deepening relationship—a trying relationship! You may have experienced love at first sight for your city, or it may have been less than love, even disdain or disgust. Maybe you were trapped, snared, captured by circumstances: a word from God, a family situation, or just going there for a little while and then moving on. A pastor's love for his city has a great deal to do with city reaching and city ministry.

The Church Call and City Call

If you were asked outright, "Do you love your church?" the answer most likely would be yes—but of course not without pain, sorrow, disappointment, glory days and gory days—but your love is real. The love for your city must be just as real and just as enduring. All cities have weaknesses and strengths, reasons people love it and hate it: the weather, traffic, population size, atmosphere, smell, ethnic mix, or educational limitations. All or any of these factors could be the reason you love or tolerate your city.

If God has called you to your church, He has called you to your city. Our vision begins not only with our church's future, but also with our city's future. When you read the newspaper or listen to the news, do you find yourself listening with no interest, no real feelings about the problems: the murders, rapes, burglaries, drownings, bankruptcies, or laws passed that are blatantly against God's Word? Does your heart response sound like this: "The world is certainly messed up. I can't believe our politicians.

There is no respect for God in our city. At least our church isn't that way. Well, let's see, what should I preach on Sunday? Ah, now this is more like it, preaching to the church."

This complacent response is exactly why many of us who are spiritual leaders need a revival in our souls concerning our love and pastoral concern for our cities. God loves the people in your church and in your city. God desires to disciple cities, shape cities, and pastor the people in our cities. We pastors and spiritual leaders have not been taught to love our cities as much as we love our churches.

Loving Your City While Loving Your Church

Permit me to share a little personal history here. My journey as a Christian leader seeking to be equipped for the ministry took me through Bible college, three seminaries, numerous conferences, seminars, and other modes of education. I have a bachelor of theology, a master of divinity from Oral Roberts University, and have done doctoral studies at Fuller Seminary and ORU. In all my hundreds of hours of classes, there was not one full-credit class on the relationship between the city and the pastor—how to love the city, pastor in the city, network in the city, be involved with city life, meet the social needs of the city, minister to the youth of the city.

Most books offer ample material for the pastor and the church on the pastoral ministry and yet never mention the pastor and the city, let alone how to reach the city. We have been somewhat trained in preaching, teaching, counseling, prayer, administration, how to study, how to speak, and how to run programs. But what happens to the city? Books abound on the subjects of ethical conduct, the pastor's wife, Sunday morning worship, midweek prayer meetings, evangelistic meetings, altar calls, dedications of infants, wedding ceremonies, funerals, ordination, finances, building programs, and praying for the sick. But what happened to the city?

Is there really any question as to why most leaders and most churches are consumed with their own churches, having little or no contact with the outside world? Why is evangelism so difficult in our twenty-first-century Church? Because we are not in the city and the city is not in us. We have removed the candlestick from the city, removed the light, the oil, the ministry of Christ in and to the city. Our first calling is not to the one congregation we preach to, but to the whole city God has placed us in.

In Luke 10:1, we read that Jesus appointed 70 leaders to go two by two into every city and place where He Himself was about to go. God has appointed you and sent you into your city because

God is coming to your city. He sent you to prepare a way for His presence and power to be released in your city. Jesus' heart for the city is revealed in Luke 19:41. Jesus is still outside of Jerusalem as He utters His lament, which only Dr. Luke records, a leader with deep feelings for his city:

> Now as He drew near, He saw the city and wept over it, saying, "If you had known, even you, especially in this your day, the things that make for your peace! But now they are hidden from your eyes. For days will come upon you when your enemies will build an embankment around you, surround you, and close you in on every side, and level you, and your children within you, to the ground; and they will not leave in you one stone upon another, because you did not know the time of your visitation" (Luke 19:41-44).

Every City Has Spiritual Seasons

Jesus was the answer Jerusalem was seeking, but Jerusalem didn't know that. Jesus was the peace this city of tension and heartache needed, but had failed to find. The very name Jerusalem meant city of peace. Its day of visitation had come but the people could not recognize it. Jesus saw beyond the day; He saw the devastation coming—the future of the city—and He wept.

As leaders sent to our cities, we must be aware that there are prophetic moments, turning points, in our cities. When the turning point is missed, the future of the city is at stake. Jesus was the prophet who could foresee and the priest intercessor who could intercede. His heart was burdened and His vision for the city would not diminish even though the future would be devastating. Every city has a future, a destiny, a hope. We are to weep with God over our city's future.

Jesus speaks emphatically about the promised visitation for the city of Jerusalem in Luke 19:44: "because you did not know the time of your visitation." The time of visitation is set by God, but must be discerned by the city leadership. The visitation would come to an indifferent city and in their indifference the people would miss the time. Their obstinate resistance to Jesus would ultimately bring the city to ruin and overthrow the entire nation. The contrast between what was and what might have been was so great that Jesus could not refrain Himself from lamentation. He wept over His city. God will visit our cities either in revival and redemptive restoration or in judgment.

Our hope is that God would come to our cities to bless, to restore, and to deliver (Gen. 21:1; 1 Sam. 2:21). Failure to know the time of visitation is followed by definite grave consequences—a spiritual deadness that cannot be remedied without a shaking, a judgment, or a time of spiritual barrenness.

Seasons of Sowing and Reaping

As a spiritual leader in my cities (we reach two cities, Portland, Oregon, and Vancouver, Washington, because they are geographically set together), I must have a heart and a vision for the visitation of God to the city. I believe the cities of today have a tremendous receptivity to the true gospel; our cities are full of opportunity. Cities, like individuals and nations, are subject to seasons—specific times to sow seed and specific times to reap the harvest.

What is the spiritual climate, the spiritual season of your city? Ted Haggard refers to the spiritual climate as knowing the water level of your city: "In the same way that water levels in a reservoir change according to the time of year or amount of rainfall, so cities and regions experience varying levels of the Holy Spirit's activity."[1]

I call this Holy Spirit activity "sowing and reaping seasons." I will reap where I have not sowed and sow where I cannot reap. It doesn't matter. What really matters is that someone reaps and reaps well at the right time. When you are pastoring for the city and not just for the church, sowing and reaping takes on a whole new perspective.

We claim Acts 18:10: "I have many people in this city." Enough people to overflow hundreds of churches by 10 times their present church size. Let us not be concerned about our own church growth but with the overall growth of the City Church. Jesus had compassion for the multitudes. City reaching is the ability to see all the people in the city in search of the living God. The multitudes are there, but can we see them? I must embrace the simple fact that if we are to reach a city, it will take the whole City Church to reach the whole city.

A Nehemiah Attitude

Each individual spiritual leader in the city must nurture a Nehemiah attitude—a passionate and persevering heart to reach our cities for God. Jerusalem was a thousand miles away from Nehemiah's world. To journey from his world, his lifestyle, and his job security through dangerous country with hostile enemies and robbers required quite a commitment from Nehemiah. Why would a man leave his comfort zone for a burned out, broken down, devastated city? The answer is that he loved his city! To leave your palace and move to a city that offers nothing but work, warfare, and weakness, you must have a vision for that city.

Nehemiah, as a city-reaching, city-restoring strategist, is a model for all leaders who have a vision for their cities. Nehemiah had a deep spiritual burden for the condition of his city and a vision to change it:

> And they said to me, "The survivors who are left from the captivity in the province are there in great distress and reproach. The wall of Jerusalem is also broken down, and its gates are burned with fire." So it was, when I heard these words, that I sat down and wept, and mourned for many days; I was fasting and praying before the God of heaven (Neh. 1:1-4).

When Nehemiah heard the state of his city, his response was four months of fasting, praying, weeping, and mourning. The biblical description of how the city was devastated by King Nebuchadnezzar is found in 2 Chronicles 36:18-20:

> And all the articles from the house of God, great and small, the treasures of the house

of the LORD, and the treasures of the king and of his leaders, all these he took to Babylon. Then they burned the house of God, broke down the wall of Jerusalem, burned all its palaces with fire, and destroyed all its precious possessions. And those who escaped from the sword he carried away to Babylon, where they became servants to him and his sons until the rule of the kingdom of Persia.

This is an accurate description of our cities today around the world. Destroyed by moral perversity, diseases, corruption, violence, the worship of other gods, idolatry, occultism, pornography, abortion, euthanasia, child molestation, spousal abuse, discouragement, suicide, poverty, and addictions—our cities have been sacked by the kingdom of darkness.

In *Loving Your City into the Kingdom*, Jack Hayford speaks of his Holy Spirit encounter during prayer when he was shown that his city was being destroyed:

> You are not being told 'Los Angeles will be destroyed,' because this city is *already* being destroyed. It does not need a catastrophic disaster to experience destruction because the Destroyer is already at work. The toll you have recounted, which a severe earthquake might cost, is small in comparison to the reality that stalks this city every day.
>
> *More* than mere thousands are being speared through by the shafts of hell's darts, seeking to take their souls. *More* than 150,000 homes (not merely houses) are being assailed by the sin and social pressures that rip families and marriages apart. *More* havoc is being wreaked by the invisible grindings of evil power than tectonic plates

could ever generate. A liquefaction of the spiritual foundations that alone allow a society to stand is wiping out the underpinnings of relationships, of righteous behavior and of healthy lifestyle.

You are to pray against THIS—the present, ongoing, devastating destruction of the city of Los Angeles.[2]

But God is not going to allow these cities to continue under the principalities and powers of evil. God is raising up Nehemiahs who will leave the world of religious matters, job security, running church programs, and running church committees to rebuild the city.

Nehemiah's response to the challenge of reaching a city was prayer and fasting. Always begin with prayer and fasting. Before we strategize, before we program, before we engage the enemy—pray!

Nehemiah was tested, attacked, accused, and faced with impossible odds; yet without delay or distraction, he finished the work of rebuilding the city (Neh. 6:15). Don't let the enemy use people as distractions to get you off course. Stay on course with your eye on the goal—the city. Nehemiah was able to unite the people of God to work together in the reaching of the city

The City Church must work together to impact a city, every congregation building on different parts of the wall, every congregation standing next to, with, along side of, and together in our ministry to the city. The knitting together of the leaders' hearts is first, then the congregations' hearts, and finally a unified city ministry can take place. We must pray that the Holy Spirit will touch the eyes of the City Church to see this vision of unified city. The Church can change the city instead of the city changing the Church.

City Church Proclamations

As a City Church, our desire to reach the city together necessitates City Church goals. The following are proclamations to make:

- As a City Church, our desire is to build strong and spiritually healthy local churches with spiritual armories so together we can penetrate the spiritual powers over our city.

  The Lord has opened His armory, and has
  brought out the weapons of His indignation;
  for this is the work of the Lord God of hosts
  in the land of the Chaldeans (Jer. 50:25).

- As a City Church, our desire is to reap the harvest God would grant us from our city metro area and region, using every means available or necessary to accomplish this.

  Then He said to His disciples, "The harvest truly is plentiful, but the laborers are few. Therefore pray the Lord of the harvest to send out laborers into His harvest"

(Matt. 9:37,38).

- As a City Church, our desire is to mobilize all believers throughout our city and region to pray, fast, prayer-walk, and unite together to minister mercy to every house, apartment, and business within our targeted area, thus reaching our whole city.

   He who sins is of the devil, for the devil has sinned from the beginning. For this purpose the Son of God was manifested, that He might destroy the works of the devil (1 John 3:8).

- As a City Church, our desire is to penetrate every pocket or stronghold of darkness by increasing our repentance, first denying all sins revealed and then increasing our power of prayer intercession over our city and region (Gen. 18:22, 23; Isa. 59:16).

> So I sought for a man among them who would make a wall, and stand in the gap before Me on behalf of the land, that I should not destroy it; but I found no one (Ezek. 22:30).

- As a City Church, our desire is to help restore the inner city by reaching individuals with the gospel of Christ, seeing authentic conversions that result in new lifestyles and new life habits and rebuilding inner City Churches that will reap and keep the harvest.

> Those from among you shall build the old waste places; you shall raise up the foundations of many generations; and you shall be called the Repairer of the Breach, the Restorer of Streets to Dwell In (Isa. 58:12).

- As a City Church, our desire is to oppose abortion, moral perversity, homosexuality, pornography, prostitution (all moral sins that violate God's laws) by being salt and light with political involvement as is necessary, taking responsibility for our city region laws, not by political activism only, but by aggressive intercession.

Son of man, I have made you a watchman for the house of Israel; therefore hear a word from My mouth, and give them warning from Me (Ezek. 3:17).

Ted Haggard speaks wisely in his book *Primary Purpose* about Christians and political involvement:

I believe that as responsible citizens, Christians should be involved in political issues. Even though we will be divided on most issues, there will be times when we will stand together. Some battles we will win, others we will lose. But the battle that must not be lost is the eternal struggle to liberate individuals spiritually, which will result in inspiring the whole community. In the midst of any political situation, we must stay steady and keep focused on our primary purpose, making it hard to go to hell from our cities.[3]

- As a City Church, our desire is to reach each generation with the power of the gospel, reaching past, present, and future generations with relevant spiritual tools and methods, we commit to raising up young leadership who will take significant leadership roles in reaching our city region.

  Now when Abram heard that his brother was taken captive, he armed his three hundred and eighteen trained servants who were born in his own house, and went in pursuit as far as Dan (Gen. 14:14).

- As a City Church, our desire is to be knit together as one corporate, unified spiritual net making up the City Church, a network of covenantal relationships governed by covenantal relationships that will catch a great amount of fish, but the net won't break.

> Now I plead with you, brethren, by the name of our Lord Jesus Christ, that you all speak the same thing, and that there be no divisions among you, but that you be perfectly joined together in the same mind and in the same judgment (1 Cor. 1:10).

- As a City Church, our desire is to turn the tide of wickedness to righteousness. We desire a full-blown authentic revival to cover our city, resulting in new conversion growth in every Bible-believing, Jesus-centered church. We are believing that our prayers and presence will change the future of our city.

> Cry aloud, spare not; lift up your voice like a trumpet; tell My people their trans-

gression, and the house of Jacob their sins (Isa. 58:1).

As a City Church consisting of many congregations, we have a great future if we will see the vision and work God's plan. The challenge far exceeds our ability to meet the needs, change the spiritual climate, and reach every house for Christ. This is precisely why a prayer intercession revival is occurring right now. Intercession is the force that touches the heart that moves the hand that changes the world. Our cities can and will be reached by a powerful Christ who is lord over the city. Let us begin with prayer:

Father,

In the Name of Jesus, let Thy Kingdom come,
let Thy will be done in our cities and regions.
We stand against the evil influences that are
warring against our region. We pray against
the spirits of rebellion, religious deception,
blasphemy, immorality, and witchcraft. Father
God, release Your warring angels and release
the Holy Spirit to do warfare against these
enemies. Set this region free; establish Your
rule and reign in our cities. Cause revival fires
to burn hot in Your church. Send revival to
this region. Release a spirit of repentance. Fill
your church with compassion and mercy. Let
the spirit of prayer intercession rest upon all
congregations. Let us, by Your grace, make a
difference in our generation. In Jesus' mighty
name, we pray.

Amen.

Personal Application

1. Do you love your city? How concerned have you been with the crime, social issues and laws there? Have you ever considered praying through your city's phone book or praying through the headlines of your local newspaper?

2. Do you have a Nehemiah attitude? Do you pray, fast, weep and mourn over your city? If not, will you commit to a set time each month for prayer with fasting over your city?

3. Are you a part of a City Church. If not, will you initiate one? If so, will you begin to declare the City Church proclamations presented in this chapter?

NOTES

1. Ted Haggard, *Primary Purpose* (Lake Mary, FL: Creation House, 1995), p. 76.

2. Ted Haggard and Jack W. Hayford, *Loving Your City into the Kingdom* (Ventura, CA: Regal Books, 1997), p. 14.

3. Ted Haggard, *Primary Purpose* (Lake Mary, FL: Creation House, 1995), p. 51.

Part 2:

KEYS TO THE CITY

The misplacement of my keys is an ongoing saga at the Damazio house. My wife of 30 years does not panic when she hears my frustrated self-murmuring, "What did I do with those keys? I am sure someone has taken them—one of the children, no doubt!"

She offers a few comments, usually something such as, "Well, this is certainly the first time Dad has lost his keys! What must we do to solve this mystery? Where will they be found?" And then, the worst happens: She heads directly for the spot where the keys have been misplaced. How humiliating! But without the keys, the car doesn't go, the office doesn't open, and private entryways become forbidden access.

The Keys to the City

And the Lord said to Joshua: "See! I have given Jericho into your hand." —Joshua 6:2

As Joshua faced Jericho, he needed the keys for entrance to the city. He did not know what the key looked like, nor could he find the key to Jericho without the locksmith—in this case, the angel of the Lord.

Every city has entry points, doors that are locked securely by the underworld's invisible forces. We need a locksmith. We need the master key. Jesus said in Matthew 16:19: "I will give you the keys of the kingdom of heaven, and whatever you bind on earth will be bound in heaven, and whatever you loose on earth will be loosed in heaven."

The keys have been given to the Church. This statement may sound very elementary, but it is, in fact, foundational to every city-reaching activity. The Church is the vehicle God has chosen to use as His keys for unlocking the doors and gates of the cities. Keys are to be used to shut what is open or open that which is locked. The Keeper of the Keys has the power to open and to shut; this power denotes God-given authority, authority that has been given to the Church.

The city has been given into the hands of the Church in the city—not to one particular church, but to the whole Church in the city. When we speak of city reaching, it is always in the context of a unified majority of the Church in a city working together to reach the entire city. Thus, the enemy works hard to keep the Church in the city divided, fragmented, isolated, and polarized. Fears, intimidation, competitive attitudes, insecurities, and carnalities are used by demonic forces to ensure that the Church does not find the keys to the city. But Scripture tells us that Jesus desires to give us the key of David that opens shut cities:

> "And to the angel of the church in Philadelphia write, 'These things says He who is holy, He who is true, He who has the key of David, He who opens and no one shuts, and shuts and no one opens: I know your works. See, I have set before you an open door, and no one can shut it; for you have a little strength, have kept My word, and have not denied My name'" (Rev. 3:7, 8).

God Gives the Right Key and the Right Approach

Our cities have been securely shut up, locked, bolted, and declared off-limits by our enemy. But Jericho was not impregnable, and Jericho was not built to withstand the army that possessed the right key and the right approach. The key may seem insulting to human reasoning; it may even be mocked by human intellect, or for that matter, rejected by a carnal program-driven church that can't see anything outside its own programs. However, the keys will be given to the humble, the intercessors of the city, the servant-driven churches.

The religious community is sometimes like the Pharisees of old who took away the key of knowledge (Luke 11:52), not going in themselves and even hindering those who might try to enter in. Our cities have already been given to us by the work of Christ on the cross and promises in God's Word. We have doors ready to open for us:

For a great and effective door has opened to me, and there are many adversaries (1 Cor. 16:9).

The integrity and fates of cities are mentioned often throughout the Bible:

- Each city has its own unique city personality and city destiny, as did the seven cities of the Roman province of Asia addressed in Revelation. The church in the city of Thyatira, for instance, was warned of its tolerance for immoral teaching:

  I know your deeds, your love and faith, your service and perseverance. . . . Nevertheless, I have this against you: You tolerate that woman Jezebel, who calls herself a prophetess. By her teaching she misleads my servants into sexual immorality and the eating of food sacrificed to idols (Rev. 2: 19-20; see also Rev. 2–3).

- Each city has its own cry that ascends to heaven—God hears that cry.

    Then the Lord said, "The outcry against Sodom and Gomorrah is so great and their sin so grievous that I will go down and see if what they have done is as bad as the outcry that has reached me. . . ." (Gen. 18:20-21; see also Isa. 14:3).

- God measures, limits, and judges the integrity of each city.

    Then Jesus began to denounce the cities in which most of his miracles had been performed, because they did not repent. "Woe to you, Korazin! Woe to you, Bethsaida! If the miracles that were performed in you had been performed in Tyre and Sidon, they would have repented long ago in sackcloth and ashes. But I tell you, it will be more bearable

for Tyre and Sidon on the day of judgment than for you." (Matt. 11:20-22; see
also Matt. 11:22-24; 23:35-38).

- God uses various means to speak clearly to
each city.

   Listen! The Lord is calling to the city—and
   to fear your name is wisdom—"Heed the
   rod and the One who appointed it" (Micah
   6:9; see also Prov. 1:20, 21; 8:1-7).

- God prepares, anoints, and sends specific ministries to specific cities.

   The word of the Lord came to Jonah
   son of Amittai: "Go to the great city of
   Nineveh and preach against it, because
   its wickedness has come up before me"
   (Jonah 1:2; see also Luke 9:51-56).

- God has a master key for each individual city.

   Now when I went to Troas to preach
   the gospel of Christ and found that the

Lord had opened a door for me (2 Cor. 2:12; see also John 4; Acts 14:27).

- God sets the Church to stand in the gap and intercede for the city.

    But Moses sought the favor of the Lord his God. "O Lord," he said, "why should your anger burn against your people, whom you brought out of Egypt with great power and a mighty hand?. . . . Turn from your fierce anger; relent and do not bring disaster on your people. . . . Then the Lord relented and did not bring on his people the disaster he had threatened. (Exod. 32:11-14; see also Ezek. 9:1-7; 22:30, 37).

- God deals with the Church about how it relates to the city. Through the apostle John, he sent a message to the church in the Roman city of Philadelphia:

These are the words of him who is holy and true, who holds the key of David. What he opens no one can shut, and what he shuts no one can open. I know your deeds. . . I know that you have little strength, yet you have kept my word and have not denied my name. (Rev. 3: 7-8; see also Rev. 2—3).

- God holds the elders of the city responsible for its spiritual state.

But if a man hates his neighbor and lies in wait for him, assaults and kills him, and then flees to one of these cities, the elders of his town shall send for him, bring him back from the city, and hand him over to the avenger of blood to die (Deut. 19:11-12; see also Daniel 21:1-9; Ezek. 3:17-21; 33:1-9).

- God weeps over the city's spiritual destiny.

> As he approached Jerusalem and saw
> the city, he wept over it (Luke 19:41).

The previous observations are very clear concerning God's burden for and involvement with the cities of our world. The keys are available, but only to the Church in the city, the true Church as described in Matthew 16:16-18:

> Simon Peter answered and said, "You are the Christ, the Son of the living God." Jesus answered and said to him, "Blessed are you, Simon Bar-Jonah, for flesh and blood has not revealed this to you, but My Father who is in heaven. And I also say to you that you are Peter, and on this rock I will build My church, and the gates of Hades shall not prevail against it."

One Church, Many Congregations

The Church in the city refers to the whole

Church, no matter what denominational or non-denominational title it may hold. All congregations that are biblically consistent with the New Testament definition of the Church make up the Church in the city. Not national or international, denominational or nondenominational, sectarian or non-sectarian—the Church is one new man, one body, and one people.

Bob Beckett says:

But this brings us to a major weakness Satan has taken advantage of since the days of Paul and Apollos: disunity among believers. Paul vented a bit of exasperation at the young Corinthian church for being divided over its preference of religious leaders in 1 Corinthians 1:10: 'Now I plead with you, brethren, by the name of our Lord Jesus Christ, that you all speak the same thing, and that there be no divisions among you.'

How much farther along are we who are on the brink of the twenty-first century than believers in first-century Corinth? If we judge our progress by the unity demonstrated today in the Body of Christ, it would seem that we have not gained much understanding in the past two thousand years![1]

The Church Jesus speaks of in Matthew 16:16-18 is the Church universal—the Church used in terms of God's general and overall plan for the whole of humanity and the universe. In Matthew 16:16-18, Jesus speaks of the local congregation as His Church. The church, when used in relation to a local body of believers, speaks to us of actual people who form a concrete expression of the manifestation of the universal Church. One is abstract, the other is concrete; one is mystical, the other is tangible; one is universal, the other is local.

The City Church is made up of many Christ-led congregations or local churches. This is a biblical model and one that is easily followed in the New Testament. Every local church must have its own eldership, personality, and focus, but in all that we do, we should seek to glorify God and work together as one Church.

Each local congregation has at least four particular identifiable marks:

- **Each Church Has Its Own Divine Destiny**

  The divine destiny is facilitated by the type of overseeing leadership the Lord places over each local congregation. The gifts of the overseeing pastor will have great influence upon the vision of that particular church. The church may take on an apostolic, evangelistic, pastoral, teaching, or prophetic spiritual chemistry according to the gift-mix of the leader.

In every city these different types of churches can be discerned. We may describe a church as an Antioch church because of its apostolic church-planting nature, a Jerusalem church because of its teaching focus, a Corinthian church because of its focus on the gifts of the Spirit, or an Ephesus church because of its regional influence, apostolic doctrine, and world focus.

- **Each Local Church Has Its Own Unique Personality**

  A church's personality is the unique methods, procedures, philosophy, and style of the local church. Personality is not the doctrinal or concrete biblical essence of the church; it is the freedom found within that church to apply and pursue truth through its own unique methods. No two families do everything the same. They may both celebrate birthdays, holidays, and special family occasions, but how they celebrate is very different. To promote unity and to assure variety at the same time, we must give room for church personality within our City Church. We all love God and worship God, but this is done not according to hard-core biblical guidelines only but also according to church personality.

Hymns or choruses, fast or slow, contemporary or traditional, short or long sermons, prayer offered silently or with plenty of joyful noises—the Bible allows for a variety of expressions. We must be on guard not to judge others' personalities as nonbiblical because they don't fit ours. Let us not meddle in other church's affairs, because in reality things are often very different than they appear from our perspective. The Scripture compares intruding in other people's affairs to grabbing an angry dog by his ears (Prov. 26:17); you will be bitten whether you hang on or let go.

- **Each Local Church Has Its Own Dominant Biblical Distinctives**

  Distinctives are usually a practical outworking of the church leadership's vision and mission established over a long period of time. Distinctives and vision values are nurtured by continual feeding upon the Word of God by the leadership team. These distinctives vary from church to church and, again, can be a source of discord and doubt among City Churches.

  Evangelistic, family focused, worship centered, teaching based, missions minded, city-prayer concentrated, social-causes oriented, leadership-training focused—all of these distinctives are rarely found in one church. We all have our focus points. If local churches would minister to the city as one Church, one Body, we would probably have all the distinctives needed in our corporate City Church to supernaturally impact the city.

- **Each Local Church Has a Responsibility to Fulfill a Unique God-Given Vision and Mission**

The vision of a local church is a reflection of its doctrinal and biblical distinctives, its own specific church history and its present leadership. Each local church vision will be different— not wrong or sub-Bible because it's not like the church you go to, just different. Chuck Swindoll offers some sound advice on answering the question, Why are we in existence as a local church?

> The array of possible answers might be: to present the gospel to the lost, to bring hope to the hurting, to provide a place of worship and instruction, to equip saints for the work of the ministry, to comfort the grieving, to feed the

hungry, to help the needy. While all of these are certainly worthwhile reasons and part of the greater picture, they are not the primary reasons for the Church's existence. The answer is "to glorify the Lord our God."[2]

Clearly all churches have this basic mandate: to glorify God. This is our mission statement, our purpose, and our vision. Undoubtedly we should desire to be as blessed and as big as God will allow us to become and to achieve as much as He will permit. Scripture clearly shows that whatever part of God's purpose we fail to complete will be a matter for personal judgment at the judgment seat of Christ (1 Cor. 3:10-15).

Conversely, there is no virtue in trying to do more than God has commanded or in struggling to be more than He has made us to be. It is enough for each church to simply fulfill the Father's plan, whether that confines us to comparative obscurity or carries us to astonishing renown (Prov. 23:4, 5; 25:27; Eccles. 4:6). Our vision must first be deeply rooted in bringing glory to God, focused upon Christ and His work, and carried out by obedience.

God has a key for the City Church to unlock every city. Like Joshua, we face our securely shut up cities, but not without divine directions from the Lord of Hosts. In the Old Testament, the people of God faced many walled cities with a warrior king and armies residing inside. In the natural, there was no way to penetrate these impregnable cities except by divine revelation, the God key. With God's key, we can open cities and turn them around.

Personal Application

1. Do you have a "City Church" mind-set, or are you in competition with and isolated from the other churches in your city? If you are not connected

with other churches, are you willing to be used as God's key for unlocking the disunity in your city?

2. Have you grabbed an angry dog by his ears lately? In other words, have you been critical of other churches that do not "do church" the way you do? Have you spread spiritual rabies by backbiting those who are different from you?

3. Whatever part of God's purpose we fail to complete will be a matter for personal judgment. What is your purpose? If you cannot define your purpose, will you spend some time in prayer with fasting to gain a vision of the purpose for your life, your church, and your city? Write out your purpose statement and keep it before you at all times.

4. Whose leadership role is being glorified by your life—God's or your own? Have you been fulfilling your own need to be recognized, or are you content to glorify God at any cost?

NOTES

1. Bob Beckett, *Commitment to Conquer* (Grand Rapids: Chosen Books, 1997), pp. 116, 117.

2. Chuck Swindoll, *The Church Purpose, Profile and Priorities* (Fullerton, CA: Insight for Living, 1987), p. 2.

Part 3:

SECURING BORDERS AND RECLAIMING OUR CITIES

*We have a strong city; God makes salvation
its walls and ramparts.*—Isaiah 26:1

Most cities worldwide are filled with violence, drugs, gangs, prostitution, poverty, and perversion, but this is not God's intention for these cities. And yet God works through faith. Therefore we must ask ourselves: What do we expect God to do in our cities? Is our vision too small? Too big? God will be to us only as big as what we expect of Him in time and space. We must begin to claim biblical promises and preach biblical hope if we are to expect biblical results. The city will be effectively influenced by the power of the gospel because the city is people, and people can be and will be reached either by the kingdom of God or the kingdom of Satan.

Our strategy must be one birthed in the spiritual realm and implemented strategically by spiritual means; natural carnal means will not accomplish spiritual ends. We must reach our cities by understanding the spiritual realm. First the spiritual, then the natural. First we take our territory by spiritual invasion, then through natural channels. As this happens, the transformed church begins to think like and function like a New Testament church. The transformed homes begin to think like and function like homes with a purpose, reaching every person with the gospel of Christ.

Prayer, Our Spiritual Firepower

One of the first steps to establishing a city-reaching church atmosphere is to establish a prayer intercession priority in the church, in every believer and, ultimately, in the whole City Church. Prayer intercession for the city will grow out of a prayer spirit that is nurtured and strengthened continually within each local congregation. To think that we have any chance at all to touch our cities without becoming powerful in prayer is ludicrous. Our prayer power will be the power that breaks down the spiritual strongholds in our churches, then in our cities. We will not be spiritually able to secure the borders of our cities until we can secure the borders in our own congregations. George Otis, Jr. explains:

> The second core factor in community transformation is fervent, united prayer. In each of our featured case studies, breakthroughs occurred when intercessors ad-

dressed specific concerns in common cause. Many of these group efforts took on their own unique identities. In Cali, Columbia, 60,000 intercessors held all-night vigils and circled the city in mobile prayer caravans. In Kampala, Uganda, hand-holding prayer warriors referred to their daily disciples as the wailing wall. In Kiambu, Kenya, believers petitioned God from a store basement that they dubbed the prayer care. Their successes led to subsequent intercessory campaigns such as Morning Glory and Operation Prayer Storm.[1]

The power for spiritually penetrating the darkness in our cities is the power of red-hot intercessory prayer.

Our Church's Intercessory Prayer Pilgrimage

As our church moved toward a clearer vision

for our city, my first assignment from the Lord was to build a greater firepower of prayer. This I systematically set out to accomplish through teaching and equipping our church in every level of prayer that I could discern from Scripture.

The first level was personal prayer. Again, before we go to war against city principalities, we should be trained in the discipline of personally touching God through prayer. We took Hosea 10:12 as our prayer text and spent many weeks going through each word:

> Sow for yourselves righteousness; reap in mercy; break up your fallow ground, for it is time to seek the LORD, till He comes and rains righteousness on you.

The series was titled "The Seven Power Points of Prayer," and our goal was to build a stronger, deeper, more powerfully alive personal prayer life in the congregation before we set out to build prayer intercession for the city. We prayed Saint Augustine's prayer as our hearts' cry:

> Oh Lord, the house of my soul is narrow;
> enlarge it, that You may enter in. I confess it,
> I know, but what shall cleanse it, to whom
> shall I cry out but to You? Cleanse me from
> my secret faults, Oh Lord, and spare Your
> servant from strange sins.[2]

Our desire was to enlarge the soul of each individual through prayer, desiring to enflame the passions of the heart for prayer, teaching the church to break up the fallow ground of the heart, plow it, and sow it with a prayer spirit.

The Seven Power Points of Prayer

We used the following outline for "The Seven Power Points of Prayer" based on Hosea 10:12:

1. The Preparation of Prayer—*"Break up"*

    Prayer begins with a heart and mind that have

been softened and planted with the Word of God. "Breaking up" the soil of our hearts refers to a personal commitment to confession and repentance.

2. The Hindrances of Prayer—*"Fallow ground"*

   The condition of our hearts determines our growth, our fruitfulness, and our destinies in God. Even as there are different conditions of physical soil, so there are different heart conditions that must be discerned in order to bring forth great fruitfulness in the spiritual realm.

3. The Urgency of Prayer—*"For it is time"*

   We live in the glorious "now" of God. The whole of time is God's arena to work on behalf of and through His faithful ones. He desires that His people be mighty in prayer, experienced in getting answers to prayer, and undisturbed by the most complex or long-standing needs.

4. The Focus of Prayer—*"To seek the Lord"*

   It is time to seek the Lord. Seeking prayer is an earnest, continual perseverance birthed from a deep hunger and drive. Seeking prayer is prayer that is Holy Spirit initiated and, through intercession, finds God's will and God's answers.

5. The Persistence of Prayer—*"Till"*

   Many prayers are granted by God but given up by the ones praying because they stopped praying before the answer came. Without the dynamic of persistence, much prayer remains unanswered.

6. The Dynamic Presence of Christ in Prayer—*"He comes"*

   Power in prayer comes from the empowering of the Holy Spirit within us. As we use that power in prayer, He continues to empower us for prayer and breathe His Spirit in us.

7. The Abundant Answers to Prayer—*"Rains righteousness on you"*

The rain of God is symbolic of God's favor, blessings, strength, and prosperity. It is prayer that both releases the rain of God and allows us to receive the rain of God.

Prayer is a vital, essential part of preparing a city-reaching church. Prayer is vital to all God's people for the advancement of the Kingdom. All the congregations must become skilled if we are to spiritually change the climate of the city. God desires all of us to be mighty in prayer, experienced in receiving answered prayer, and unmoved in persevering in the most complex or long-standing needs. As we can see from the following verses, when this holy, fervent flame of prayer is lit, the soul awakens the interest of heaven, attracts the attention of God, and places at the disposal of those who exercise it the exhaustless riches of grace:

Let us therefore come boldly to the throne of grace, that we may obtain mercy and find grace to help in time of need (Heb. 4:16).

Let my prayer be set before You as incense, the lifting up of my hands as the evening sacrifice (Ps. 141:2).

Church Service Intercession

We established a prayer focus that encouraged a new level of prayer in each individual believer and then raised the level of corporate prayer. For many years, prior to every service, we had what we called "Pre-Service Prayer," a 30-minute corporate prayer time in a room other than our sanctuary. This corporate prayer time had been successful in keeping a prayer focus, but not everyone was consistently committed to coming one-half hour before the service.

To extend our prayer atmosphere goal, we moved our corporate all-church prayer time into the weekend services. We have all-church prayer at different times during our normal weekend services. Sometimes at the beginning of the service we will open with unified prayer, or proclamation prayer, cleansing prayer, small groups praying together, lifting hands and praying, or joining hands for agreement prayer. We may have a prayer time during the worship service, at the end of worship service, or during the preaching time. I may lead the whole church into a prayer session. Our goal is to expose the entire congregation on a weekly basis to the power of prayer intercession.

At that time, we scheduled a 12-month preaching focus on intercessory prayer based on Ezekiel 22:30:

So I sought for a man among them who would make a wall, and stand in the gap before Me on behalf of the land, that I should not destroy it; but I found no one.

The series was entitled "Gap Standing and Hedge Building: Responding to the Call of the Spirit to Become a Church of Intercession." Our goal was to motivate the entire congregation into a deeper level of prayer intercession that would release the supernatural power of God in an obvious and awesome manner, resulting in overwhelming harvest.

Intercessory prayer is the single most important of all ministries in the church. Prayer creates an expectant, heavenly-charged atmosphere and binds the power of darkness so the gospel can go forward and the Church can prosper. Intercessory prayer is the sign of a person's soul expanding, deepening, and becoming like Christ in compassion and mercy. Without intercessory prayer, the protective hedge around our borders may be broken down, allowing easy access for the enemy to come in to destroy people, homes, marriages, families, spiritual life, and health both in our churches and our cities. Corporate intercessory prayer has incredible power to change "what is" to "what can be" by the power and grace of God, in spite of whatever obstacles appear to be hindering the church (Exod. 8:28; Isa. 59:16; Jer. 27:18; Rev. 5:8; 8:3, 4).

Our Prayer Sequence

You don't start with cities and nations first. You must first establish power and momentum before taking on the city. The whole church becomes a prayer intercession instrument and then special focus areas are taken on by the specialized intercessors. We have a seven-day-a-week Prayer Center (as of this writing, there are more than 2,000 churches with Prayer Centers), a Prayer Pastor, a Prayer Center Overseer, Prayer Teams for every staff pastor, Prayer Teams for each service, prayer during the service, and a variety of prayer teams. The following list provides a more detailed, but not complete, picture of our prayer foundation:

- **Ministry Team Intercessors:** Intercessors who minister during services at altar calls, over water baptism candidates, and pray for healing and urgent needs. These intercessors must be approved by an elder or pastor and function with the laying on of hands.

- **Service Intercessors:** A scheduled core of intercessors—but open to any intercessor—who meet during the Sunday morning service behind the stage, with audio-visual reception of the service. Prayer focuses on that Sunday's message.

- **Third Row Intercessors:** Scheduled intercessors sit in the third row behind the pastors' pew during all services. Throughout the service, they focus on praying for me, my family, the MC, and guest speakers.

- **Pre-Service Soaking Prayer:** Open to anyone interested in receiving soaking prayer prior to the Sunday evening service. Ministry Team Intercessors are available to soak anyone desiring prayer, such as visiting ministry, worship teams, water baptismal candidates, STORM Teams, et cetera. Two or three intercessors also pray over every seat in the sanctuary.

- **Event Engine Room Intercessors:** Intercessors who meet backstage to pray prior to and during special events, such as the Eternity Production, conference, retreats.

- **Event Intercessors:** Intercessors who pray in their homes for the participants in special events, such as the Eternity Production, STORM Teams, Tapestry Teams, conferences, and children's productions, before, during, and after the event.

- **City Care Prayer Warriors:** Intercessors who pray in their homes receive weekly prayer lists taken from the pew information cards and pray for church visitors, their prayer requests, and church members' prayer requests.

- **Departmental Armor Bearers:** Intercessors who are assigned to cover different departments throughout church. They pray in their homes and meet at specific times in the Prayer Center to pray with members of those departments.

- **Healing Prayer:** Intercessors and those needing physical healing meet in the Prayer Center weekly for a brief time of teaching before praying for the sick.

- **Daniel Prayer Intercessors:** Intercessors who meet in the Prayer Center to intercede specifically for spiritual breakthrough in our city, state, and nation.

- **Deborahs Arise:** Intercessors who meet in our Prayer Center to pray for our prodigals.

- **Personal Armor Bearers:** Intercessors who are a part of specific teams chosen by elders and department heads to pray for them, their families, and ministries. The intercessors pray in their homes and meet at specific times to pray for their leaders with the laying on of hands.

- **Prayer Guard:** Intercessors who pray daily in their homes at a secondary level for leaders, their families, and ministries as assigned. They do not meet with the leader.

- **Threefold Cord Intercessors:** Intercessory groups, consisting of three individuals or three couples, who agree to pray together for one another on a consistent basis.

- **Downtown Intercessors:** Intercessors who meet weekly downtown in the Justice Center to pray and prayer-walk the business and city government districts.

- **Strategic City Taking Intercessors:** Intercessors who meet on Friday evening for Spirit-led "times of war" with prayer that is focused on Portland and Vancouver.

- **Pray Portland:** An hour-long radio program every Sunday morning from 6:00 to 7:00 A.M. Teams of eight intercessors pray for the City of Portland on the air consecutively for 60 minutes.

- **Northwest Prayer Watch:** Intercessors who meet in the Prayer Center to pray for the harvest and prayer requests from the churches of the Northwest: Oregon, Washington, and Idaho.

Our broad foundation of praying people allows us to focus on the city with prayer intercession that cannot be intimidated, outflanked, or counterattacked without knowing what's happening. We are more prepared for a wider variety of spiritual warfare because we are more broadly equipped. Our Opening Service Intercession involves prayer for personal cleansing, personal enlargement, renewal of the heart, Holy Spirit empowerment, and prayer for our city. We pray against specific spiritual strongholds in our region; we pray for the lost; and we pray for revival. This opening intercession will last about 20 minutes and flows into a worship time. (I discuss the whole topic of prayer intercession individually, corporately, and for our cities in the book *Seasons of Intercession.*[3])

Establishing God's Perimeters

The prayer anointing is absolutely essential to reaching our cities by tearing down spiritual strongholds, piercing the darkness, and setting the captives free. Realizing that our city was notorious for New Age material, pornography, euthanasia, legalizing medical marijuana, worshiping mother earth, and several other obvious strongholds, we decided to spiritually claim our borders.

Ed Silvoso says that the first step to reaching an entire city for Christ is to establish God's perimeters in the city. In military science a perimeter is the outer boundary of an area where defenses are set up. The term implies a warfare context, real or potential.[4] I would say the warfare is real! That's one very good reason why you need prayer power before you start assaulting the enemy.

When we moved toward a strategy to reach our city, we moved into another level of spiritually intense warfare. We chose to stake out the Northeast/Southeast section of our city that represented more than 800,000 of our 1.5 million metro area population. I asked several pastors in our city with whom we have a relationship and who are representative of a broad section of the City Church in the Northeast and Southeast areas to join with us.

Baptist, Independent, Evangelical, Pentecostal, Charismatic, and Foursquare pastors were involved—Caucasian, African-American, and Hispanic. Together we set out to do what we simply called Reclaiming Our Borders, a spiritual proclamation. We mapped out our route and made wooden stakes with appropriate Scriptures written on each one of them. Then we set out to claim our borders in three vans. The first van was packed with pastors, the second and third van were filled with very noisy intercessors. The scriptures we put on the stakes were Psalms 46:1-5; 48:2, 3; 68:3-11; 107:6-8; Proverbs 11:11; Isaiah 1:26; 26:1-7; 33:20, 21; 54:2-5; 58:11, 12; 62:11, 12; Matthew 16:16-19; Acts 18:9, 10. We claimed the following border scriptures:

> David also defeated Hadadezer the son of Rehob, king of Zobah, as he went to recover his territory at the River Euphrates (2 Sam. 8:3).
> The lines have fallen to me in pleasant plac-

es; yes, I have a good inheritance (Ps. 16:6).

You have set all the borders of the earth; you have made summer and winter (Ps. 74:17).

And He brought them to His holy border, this mountain which His right hand had acquired. He also drove out the nations before them, allotted them an inheritance by survey, and made the tribes of Israel dwell in their tents (Ps. 78:54, 55).

He makes peace in your borders, and fills you with the finest wheat (Ps. 147:14).

Even though Edom has said, "We have been impoverished, but we will return and build the desolate places," thus says the Lord of hosts: "They may build, but I will throw down; they shall be called the Territory of Wickedness, and the people against whom the LORD will have indignation forever" (Mal. 1:4).

As we moved to each premarked staking spot, the van of intercessors followed and sustained continuous intercession during the whole event, about five hours in length. At each spot we gathered around the stake and read a prayer proclamation, then each pastor took a turn with the sledgehammer to drive the stake in the ground. Finally, we poured oil upon it, placed our feet on top of the stake, and prayed for our city borders to be reclaimed.

Our Prayer Proclamation

The prayer proclamation I wrote for the occasion is as follows:

On the basis of Scripture, we as leaders stand in the gap for our city. We pastors of Northeast and Southeast Portland stand together as representatives of other city leaders who desire to:

Repent (Dan. 9:4-9). We ask the Lord Jesus

to forgive us for sins that have taken place in our state, in our city, in our Northeast and Southeast regions. We ask forgiveness for the sins of political corruption, racial prejudice, moral perversions, witchcraft, the occult, and idolatry. We pray the blood of Jesus to cleanse our hands from shedding innocent blood in the acts of abortion, euthanasia, and any other ways the innocent have been destroyed. We ask forgiveness for divisions in the Church, for spiritual pride, for backbiting, for anything that has hurt the Church of Jesus Christ. We repent, humble ourselves, and ask for mercy to be poured out upon our land, our community, and our churches.

Request (Jer. 29:7). We ask for God's kingdom to come and His will to be done on earth as it is in heaven. We ask in the name of the Lord Jesus Christ for a spiritual out-pouring of God's grace, mercy, and fire upon our city. We ask for true spiritual revival to come to our community, causing a turning to God, a cleansing, a brokenness, a humility, a hunger for the one and only true God. God, we ask for mercy here. We ask that our destiny not be aborted. We ask that you visit our city, our churches, and our homes. Do not pass our city by. We ask for restoration of the foundations of righteousness to our city.

Resist (Eph. 6:10-17; Jas. 4:7). On the basis of our submission to God, we in faith resist the devil and his work. We resist all forces and powers of evil that have taken hold of our city. We resist the spirit of wickedness that has established strongholds in our city region—the dark places, the hidden works of darkness, the mystery places where the enemy has set up encampments. We call on the name of the Lord to destroy all spiritual strongholds. We proclaim this day that the city of Portland, especially the Northeast and Southeast regions, is now under the power and ownership of the Holy Spirit. All other spirits are hereby given notice and are evicted from this property by the power of the name of Jesus. Today we stand in the gap and rebuild a hedge of protection around our city.

We claim this day Isaiah 58:11, 12: "The LORD will guide you continually, and satisfy your soul in drought, and strengthen your bones; you shall be like a watered garden, and like a spring of water, whose waters do not fail. Those from among you shall build the old waste places; you shall raise up the foundations of many generations; and you shall be called the Repairer of the Breach, the Restorer of Streets to Dwell In."

We claim this day Isaiah 1:26: "I will restore your judges as at the first, and your counselors as at the beginning. Afterward you shall be called the city of righteousness, the faithful city."

We claim this day Matthew 16:18, 19: "And I also say to you that you are Peter, and on this rock I will build My church, and the gates of Hades shall not prevail against it. And I will give you the keys of the kingdom of heaven, and whatever you bind on earth will be bound in heaven, and whatever you loose on earth will be loosed in heaven."

Now we pray that our city will be reclaimed, restored, revived, and set on a path of righteousness. We pray that our borders will be secured on this day, January 4. May God give us grace, protect us, and allow His angels to encamp round about us. This we do in humility and faith.

Identificational Repentance

The President of Zambia, President Chiluba, prayed for his nation with what we would call identificational repentance:

Dear God, as a nation we now come to You, to Your throne of grace, and we humble ourselves and admit our guilt. We repent from all our wicked ways of idolatry, witchcraft, the occult, immorality, injustice, and corruption and other sins that have violated Your righteous laws. We turn away from all this and renounce it all in Jesus' name. We ask for forgiveness and cleansing through the blood of Jesus. Therefore, we thank You that You will heal our land. We pray that You will send healing, restoration, revival, blessing, and prosperity to Zambia.[5]

The purpose of staking the city is to geographically proclaim repentance over the city. The church is identifying with the corporate sins of the city, repenting of those sins, forsaking them, and publicly apologizing. This may not visibly solve all the problems in the city, and there may be no identifiable changes to the natural eye, but in the spiritual world, we are taking away the places the enemy has a right to invade. We are cleansing things in the invisible realm as Daniel did in Daniel 9:4-19. The sins Daniel identified with were not his personal sins; he did not commit the sins, but he did repent with and for the people. He believed God would do something for the nation if he would confess, repent, weep, and ask for cleansing.

John Dawson, a leader in identification repentance, says: "If we have broken our covenant with God and violated our relationships with one another, the path to reconciliation must begin with the act of confession."[6]

Bob Beckett gives more counsel on the subject of identificational repentance:

It is conventional in that we must seek God's forgiveness for personal sin as well as for sin committed by the Church. Without asking His forgiveness, we have no business attempting any kind of spiritual warfare. But the call to repentance is unconventional in that the object of repentance includes much more than the sins for which we as individuals are responsible. The term given to this broader expression of penitence is identificational repentance, an act by which we identify with and ask forgiveness for the sin of a group, a city, or a nation with which we are connected. Identificational repentance is a powerful weapon in our arsenal of warfare whose time has come.[7]

When we staked our city, by faith, we identified with the corporate city sins, racial injustice, worship of other gods, perversions, and immorality, and asked God to have mercy on our city by first cleansing the church. Securing the borders may seem unreal to many, down right unscriptural to some, and subjective or just plain nonsense to others. But the fact that we had more people asking Christ into their hearts in the following 12 months than at any other time in the history of our local church just might be connected to our prayers of repentance and securing our borders.

After staking our city, we met together for a City Church Communion Service with the pastors and some of their congregations at our church facility to publicly confess our sins, claim our borders, and intercede for our city. Nearly 3,000 people, pastors, and city leaders spent three hours in prayer, worship, intercession, confession, repentance, and partaking of communion together. We communicated to the congregations with a video of the city staking and a biblical statement explaining why we did this and what we expected.

Start Where You Are with As Many As You Can

Corporate intercession with the City Church pastors, elders, leaders, and congregations is a powerful tool for city intercession and city warfare. We only had a seed of representation from our whole metro area.

If you wait until you have a majority it may never happen—you have to start somewhere. It could be the city will have several different groups doing the same things at the same time and maybe in the future the groups will merge for further unified expression.

We sponsor City Pastors' Breakfasts three or four times a year with 200 to 250 out of 1,200 pastors in our city attending. The breakfasts are aimed at certain levels of prayer, unity, and city focus. We eat, we fellowship, we meet, and we introduce new pastors who have pioneered or taken over a church in our city. Then we pray for new pastors, and allow pastors to hand out "city event" communications. Finally, we worship, and usually hear from a visiting speaker. We don't push a certain strategy to reach our city, trying to get everyone on board.

We seek general unity, not specific unity. If we would have asked that group of 250 pastors to come to a place of biblical conviction and spiritual unity in the area of symbolism, spiritual subjectivity, spiritual warfare, and identificational repentance, I don't think the city staking would have happened. As a matter of fact, we might still be there discussing it! Within the larger breakfast group, I have reached out to those who seem to have the same vision and ideas for reaching our city. This group only consists of about 20 pastors who meet monthly. We pray together, open up our ministries to one another, preach at each other's churches, and help each other in any way we can.

The same principle applies to racial reconciliation: I heard it; I did it with others in large conferences and city events, but I didn't personally feel reconciled. I needed to go to another level, so I called one of the African-American pastors in our city, sat down, and said, "Teach me to understand why we need to be reconciled. What it is, and how can I change our relationship?" This contact began a series of events that caused racial reconciliation to become a reality for me, the church I pastor, and our ministry to the inner city.

As a local pastor, I still cooperate in larger city events, such as the Billy Graham Crusade, Luis Palau Crusade, City Pastor Prayer Summits, and more. I believe every pastor should find those he relates to and do what he can do to reach the city.

With all the books, articles, and conferences on city reaching that are available, you have to start somewhere. Prayer intercession with either a small or large group of pastors is a great place to start. Maybe you won't stake your city. Fine, do whatever you have to do to focus on breaking the powers of hell over your city.

Don't Neglect the Promises Already Given

Prayer intercession is recognizing and standing against evil spirits that lie behind the chronic historical problems in our cities. Through intercessory prayer, we can release the power of revival into every part of our cities with measured results seen in salvations and deliverance. Maybe you have received promises, visions, dreams, or words for your city. Dig them out and begin to intercede over them. We at City Bible Church have used several different visions and city prayers for the church of Portland as a source of prayer intercession for our city.

The following is a sampling of what we have used:

John G. Lake:

> To my amazement, on approaching the building, high in the atmosphere, half a mile or more, I discerned millions of demons, organized as a modern army. There were those who apparently acted as shock troops. They would charge with great ferocity, followed by a wave, and yet another wave, and yet another wave. After a little while, I observed there operated a restraining influence that constituted a barrier through which they could not force them-

selves. With all the ingenuity of humans at war, this multitude of demons seemed to endeavor to break the barrier or to go further, but were utterly restrained. . . . "Teach the people to pray for this. For this, and this alone, will meet the necessity of the human heart, and this alone will have the power to overcome the forces of darkness." As the angel was departing he said, "Pray. Pray. Pray. Teach the people to pray. Prayer and prayer alone, much prayer. Persistent prayer is the door of entrance into the heart of God."[8]

Frank Damazio: A Corporate Service Intercessory Prayer

If you had ears to hear in the spirit realm, you would hear thousands and millions of voices. The voices that are crying out are the voices of evil, voices of evil saying, "Give us this city! Give us the souls of these people!" If you had ears to hear, you would hear the words of the darkness crying out, "Give us this city! Give us this region!" They are pressing into the heavenlies, but they come up against an invisible force that surrounds the city. The force is the force of the prayers that are going up around the city. And as the demons press in, they can't press through, and they cry out to one another, "Where can we go to press in? Where can we go to find the way? Where can we go to make room? Where can we go to devastate?" But the angels cry back and forth, "There is no entry. There is no way. There is no path into our region." For the Lord has cried aloud through the people and through the saints of the Most High. There is a covering, a covering. You're resisting. You're holding back the demonic forces. They cannot come through. Do not let up. Do not pull back. This a day of victory, a day of hungering, a day of shattering the forces of evil. Oh, press, press, and press and press in. Press, press, for the evil forces are moving back. They are moving back. They are not penetrating. The Lord will give you total and absolute victory in your cities if you would press. Do not smite the ground once or twice, but smite the ground over and over again. Smite it until the victory is complete. Press, press, and keep on pressing through powerful Holy Spirit praying.[9]

Prayer-walking

Securing borders also involves what Steve Hawthorne and Graham Kendrick termed "prayer-walking." Prayer-walking is simply walking while praying specific, directed, intentional prayers in a very unsuspecting and non-attention-drawing way. To see our neighborhoods and workplaces as they really are, we need to add a simple ingredient: prayer-walking.

This kind of praying is seeking to release God's blessing over the area, praying that His grace, mercy, and redeeming love be released over the person or the place prayed for. Anyone and everyone can accomplish this type of on-site praying. Prayer-walking is not new; Scripture reveals numerous examples of this kind of prayer:

Arise, walk in the land through its length and its width, for I give it to you (Gen. 13:17).

Every place that the sole of your foot will tread upon I have given you, as I said to Moses (Josh. 1:3).

Then the men arose to go away; and Joshua

charged those who went to survey the land, saying, "Go, walk through the land, survey it, and come back to me, that I may cast lots for you here before the LORD in Shiloh" (Josh. 18:8).

Prayer-walking is part of the believer's responsibility in discovering the fruit of the future, seeing our region filled with God's future blessings. As I have heard Ed Silvoso say on many occasions: "We must talk to God about our neighbor before we talk to our neighbors about God!" We need to prepare every place Jesus is about to go into. Scripture reveals the goal of prayer-walking—securing our borders:

After these things the Lord appointed seventy others also, and sent them two by two before His face *into every city and place* where He Himself was about to go. Then He said to them, "The harvest truly is great, but the laborers are few; therefore pray the Lord of the harvest to send out laborers into His harvest. Go your way; behold, I send you out as lambs among wolves" (Luke 10:1-3, *italics added*).

So Moses swore on that day, saying, "Surely the land where your foot has trodden shall be your inheritance and your children's forever, because you have wholly followed the LORD my God' (Josh. 14:9).

Prayer-walking is a practical way to secure the borders of our homes, neighborhoods, and work places. Again, it may sound childish or foolish to the Western worldview because of its lack of any interest in the invisible realm, but for those of us who see prayer-walking, claiming, staking, and anointing with oil as the tangible means for proclaiming spiritual truths, these simple actions do have powerful potential. As you read through the following verses, notice that God is very concerned with where, why, and how we walk upon this earth:

> You shall tread upon the lion and the cobra, the young lion and the serpent you shall trample underfoot (Ps. 91:13).

> And the God of peace will crush Satan under your feet shortly. The grace of our Lord Jesus Christ be with you. Amen (Rom. 16:20).

> To give light to those who sit in darkness and the shadow of death, to guide our feet into the way of peace (Luke 1:79).

> And having shod your feet with the preparation of the gospel of peace (Eph. 6:15).

The purpose of prayer-walking is to further secure your spiritual borders, bless the people and the places, intercede, stand in the gap, bind principalities and powers, clear the air, and make way for the gospel to come in power. As you prayer-walk your neighborhood, you may face a difficult challenge represented in each home. Prayer-walking is moving the church into the community (Acts 2:46, 47).

Prayer-walking earth is our heavenly intercession; it allows the people of the church to become the people of the neighborhood and the people of the city. The Holy Spirit prompts spiritual intercession with discernment that builds a perimeter of faith and secures our spiritual borders. As we practice this simple strategy for reaching our cities, we will encounter lost people and often these encounters will lead to conversions (Matt. 9:20-22; Ps. 2:8).

When we begin to secure our borders with prayer-walking intercession, we will invade Satan's territory and we will discern the evil there with a heightened sensitivity to demonic and evil forces. We will enter into territories Satan has held for long periods of time with no intruders and no confrontations. We will become God's voice and instrument to bring down these powers and establish a beachhead for the power of the gospel to go forth. Getting righteous people out on the streets of our cities in a strategic, consistent manner may be one of the most effective means to reaching an entire city. The following Scriptures assure us that prayer can change the balance of spiritual power and make our cities more prepared to receive the power of Jesus.

> By the blessing of the upright the city is exalted, but it is overthrown by the mouth of the wicked (Prov. 11:11).

> For the weapons of our warfare are not carnal but mighty in God for pulling down strongholds (2 Cor. 10:4).

As we secure the borders of our neighborhoods, cities, and states, we intercede for these places to be filled with the power of God that brings deliverance to individuals, health to families, restoration to marriages, gainful employment to the poor, wholesome recreational activities to the community, physical protection to both residents and businesses, spiritual peace to those who are confused, hunger for God to those who are apathetic toward Him, and restoration, refilling, and revival in the Holy Spirit to our churches.

Pray that the territory within the perimeter of your city will be a place where the kingdom of God advances without hindrance and Satan's strongholds are destroyed. Pray that we will become the unified, covenant-keeping, intercessory-prayer-walking, faith-talking, life-transforming Church that we are called to be. We can secure our borders; we can reclaim our cities. We must have spiritual reviving and a Holy Spirit movement within our churches. We need God!

Believe

By Donna Lasit

I say on Sunday how much I want revival

But then by Monday, I can't
even find my Bible

Where's the pow'r, the pow'r of
the cross in my life

I'm sick of playin' the game of religion

I'm tired of losing my reason for livin'

Where's the pow'r, the pow'r of
the cross in my life

I'm not content just to walk
through my life givin' in

To the lies walkin' in compromises now

We cry out as a generation that was lost

But now is found in the pow'r of the cross

We believe in You

We believe in the pow'r of Your
    Word and its truth

We believe in You

So we lay down our cause that our
    cross might be found in You

I'm not satisfied doin' it my own way

I'm not satisfied to "do church" and walk away

I'm not satisfied there's no love
    in my life but You

I'm not satisfied livin' in yesterday's hour

I'm not satisfied to have the form,
    but not the pow'r

I'm not satisfied Oh Lord I am cru-
    cified in You, in You.[10]

Personal Application

1. Prayerlessness is pridefulness; it says that we can do it without God's help. Is prayer a priority in your personal schedule? Have you made prayer a priority in your church or ministry?

2. Have you staked your neighborhood or your city to geographically proclaim repentance over the city? What corporate sins of the city do you and other leaders need to repent for, forsake and publicly apologize for?

3. What are you doing to create unity in your city? Are you willing to meet with other leaders who do not agree with you on every issue? If so, make a list of those you will contact and agree to meet for breakfast.

4. Are you willing to become God's voice and instrument to bring down the demonic powers in your city and to establish a beachhead for the

power of the gospel to go forth? Will you make a commitment to prayer-walking on a consistent basis?

NOTES

1. George Otis, Jr., *Informed Intercession* (Ventura, CA: Regal Books, 1999), p. 3. of prepublished manuscript.

2. Saint Augustine, source unknown.

3. Frank Damazio, *Seasons of Intercession* (Portland, OR: City Bible Publishing, 1998).

4. Ed Silvoso, *That None Should Perish* (Ventura, CA: 1994), p. 23.

5. John Dawson, *Healing America's Wounds* (Ventura, CA: Regal Books, 1994), p. 47.

6. Ibid., p. 29.

7. Bob Beckett, *Commitment to Conquer* (Grand Rapids: Chosen Books, 1997), p. 128.

8. John G. Lake, *His Life and Sermons* (Fort Worth: Kenneth Copeland Publications, 1994), n. p.

9. Prophetic word given by Frank Damazio at the Winter Prayer Conference, January 18, 1997 during the evening service.

10. Donna Lasit, "Believe," City Bible Music, 2000. Used with permission.

Part 4:

LEADING CITIES TO THE LIGHT

*The way of the wicked is like darkness; they
do not know what makes them stumble.*
—Proverbs 4:19

A member of our church had a vivid dream
about hell and the powers of darkness; this
dream was given to me in writing. It is as follows:

I saw hell as surrounded by a large iron
fence. Christians were patrolling the fence
and watching for those inside to come near

the fence, being drawn by the light and sounds that came from outside. As those inside approached the fence, the Christians would reach through the bars, grab the lost, and drag them through the fence into the kingdom of light. The only ones who were rescued were those who were drawn to the light, those who were free enough to be able to reach out and look for help.

Then I saw that as the Church was storming the gates of hell, the gates were knocked loose and hung open on their hinges. The Christians then marched through the gates and into the strongholds of hell. As they strode through the dark halls, they would stop at one cell after another and look at the prisoner inside. Each prisoner's body was bound tightly with one set of chains; another set chained the prisoner to the wall of the cell; the cell doors were also locked. When a Christian looked inside, he would point to a cell and declare, "That one is destined for the kingdom of God. Release him." The chains would then break free from the walls and the cell door would open. The Christian would then go to another door and say, "That one is God's. Free him." And the cell door would fly open, as the chains knocked loose. The rescued ones were led out of the dark halls, through the courtyard of hell, and into the kingdom of light.

This woman's vision could be an accurate description of the horrible bondage many people face in our cities. For so long we have been content to remain on the outskirts, rescuing those who manage to slip far enough away from the clutches of the enemy that they are lured to the light. But now it is time to march into the depths of hell and free those

who are chained in darkness and bring them out.
The covering of darkness over our cities is very real
and powerful.

Cities Without Form and Void

Genesis 1:2 describes the earth before the moving of the Spirit of God. It may also depict our cities
in desperate need of the creative power of the Holy
Spirit:

> The earth was without form, and void; and
> darkness was on the face of the deep. And
> the Spirit of God was hovering over the
> face of the waters.

In *26 Translations of the Old Testament*, exposition on the above passage reads: "And the earth was
waste and void," "unformed and void," "invisible and
unfurnished," "a formless wasteland," "chaotic," "had
existed waste and void," "a shapeless chaotic mass,"
and "darkness hung over the deep," "and darkness

was on the face of the roaring deep," "and while a mighty wind swept over the waters."[1]

If you substitute the word "city" for "earth" and read the verse out loud, you may see a direct parallel with your city: a city that is a wasteland, void, unfurnished, formless, chaotic—a shapeless mass with darkness hung over it—its only hope the hovering creative Spirit of God. Our cities are like the raging waves of a dark sea, tossing, turning, throwing themselves against the darkness—no escape, no hope, no future, unless the Spirit of God blows His creative breath over those raging waters to bring new life.

The two negative Hebrew words used in this verse for "without form" and "void" are a double expression to describe the utmost of an unformed, unshaped mass. These two Hebrew words, *tohu* and *bohu,* denote that this confused mass had remained this way, unchanged, for a long period of time.

"Without form" is the Hebrew word *tohu*, meaning to lie waste, a desolation, desert land, a worthless thing, confusion, to have no order, chaos, unformed. *Tohu* is translated in other Old Testament verses to describe a desert wasteland (Deut. 32:10; Job 6:18), a destroyed city (Isa. 24:10), a moral and spiritual emptiness with confusion (1 Sam. 12:21; Isa. 29:21, 44:9; 45:19), and a nothingness and unreality (Isa. 49:4).[2] All of these descriptions accurately describe the state of the cities we strategize to reach. The challenge is staggering—through human eyes hopeless, intimidating, and impossible. Why even start? Because our hope is in the Word of God and the supernatural power of the Holy Spirit.

Hoshek Darkness

The Hebrew word for "darkness" in Genesis 1:2 is *hoshek* which means a covering of darkness, a covering that influences everything it touches.[3] In Exodus 10:21, 22 *hoshek* refers to a darkness that can be felt, a thick darkness that covered the land:

> Then the Lord said to Moses, "Stretch out your hand toward heaven, that there may be darkness over the land of Egypt, darkness which may even be felt." So Moses stretched out his hand toward heaven, and there was thick darkness in all the land of Egypt three days.

Hoshek is a darkness that covers people's lives, influencing every part of their lives until they ultimately "sit down" under the covering of darkness:

> Those who sat in darkness and in the shadow of death, bound in affliction and irons (Ps. 107:10).

> They do not know, nor do they understand; they walk about in darkness; all the foundations of the earth are unstable (Ps. 82:5).

Hoshek is a darkness that darkens people's understanding. Their lives are filled with darkness; they sit in darkness, and they walk in darkness. Darkness brings calamity, ignorance, gloom, anguish, and oppression. Darkness has the power to drive people into more and more darkness until everything about their lives is flooded in darkness:

> Then they will look to the earth, and see trouble and darkness, gloom of anguish; and they will be driven into darkness (Isa. 8:22).
>
> I sink in deep mire, where there is no standing; I have come into deep waters, where the floods overflow me (Ps. 69:2).

Our cities are covered with *hoshek* darkness, and the people are servants to this thick, felt, driving force. The hope we have is a Genesis 1:2 hope: "And the Spirit of God was hovering over the face of the waters." As we learn the power of prayer intercession coupled with repentance and brokenness, we can believe the hovering Spirit of God for a mighty wind to sweep over our cities, forcing the state of nothingness and emptiness to surrender to the fullness of God. This does not happen, however, in one instantaneous act, but through a persistent, continuous Holy Spirit process.

Our cities do have a *hoshek* darkness, but they are ripe to receive a *ruah* (Hebrew: spirit, breath) of God to penetrate that darkness. City reaching involves darkness piercing and removing the covering of darkness from our cities so that the light of the gospel can be received. Genesis 1:4 says, "And God saw the light, that it was good; and God divided the light from the darkness." God desires to divide the darkness in our cities.

Skotta Darkness

In Greek, the word for darkness is *skotta*, *skotos* or *stokeinos* which means to be full of darkness or completely covered with darkness. This Greek word is translated "dark" in Luke 11:36 and "full of darkness" in Matthew 6:23 and Luke 11:34 where the physical condition is figurative of the moral. The group of *skot* words is derived from a root *ska* meaning to cover.4 (John 1:5; 8:12; 12:35, 46; Rom. 2:19; 1 John 1:5; 2:8, 9, 11.) This *skotta* darkness denotes a spiritual or moral darkness emblematic of sin as a condition of moral or spiritual depravity. It is a darkness that covers the city, covers the people, and affects every area of life:

- Darkness affects comprehension.
  And the light shines in the darkness, and the darkness did not comprehend it (John 1:5).
- Darkness affects lifestyle.
  Then Jesus spoke to them again, saying, "I am the light of the world. He who follows Me shall not walk in darkness, but have the light of life" (John 8:12).
- Darkness can overtake people.

Then Jesus said to them, "A little while longer the light is with you. Walk while you have the light, lest darkness overtake you; he who walks in darkness does not know where he is going" (John 12:35).

- Darkness can be broken.

I have come as a light into the world, that whoever believes in Me should not abide in darkness (John 12:46).

This is the message which we have heard from Him and declare to you, that God is light and in Him is no darkness at all (1 John 1:5).

- Darkness will pass away.

Again, a new commandment I write to you, which thing is true in Him and in you, because the darkness is passing away, and the true light is already shining. He who says he is in the light, and hates his brother, is in darkness until now (1 John 2:8,9).

- Darkness is strengthened through hatred.

  But he who hates his brother is in darkness and walks in darkness, and does not know where he is going, because the darkness has blinded his eyes (1 John 2:11).

  And are confident that you yourself are a guide to the blind, a light to those who are in darkness (Rom. 2:19).

- Darkness can dominate cities through evil spiritual powers.

  For we do not wrestle against flesh and blood, but against principalities, against powers, against the rulers of the darkness of this age, against spiritual hosts of wickedness in the heavenly places. Therefore take up the whole armor of God, that you may be able to withstand in the evil day, and having done all, to stand (Eph. 6:12, 13).

  Then the fifth angel poured out his bowl on the

throne of the beast, and his kingdom became full of darkness; and they gnawed their tongues because of the pain (Rev. 16:10).

- Darkness torments people through evil spirits.

But the Spirit of the LORD departed from Saul, and a distressing spirit from the LORD troubled him (1 Sam. 16:14).

And when the unclean spirit had convulsed him and cried out with a loud voice, he came out of him (Mark 1:26).

And always, night and day, he was in the mountains and in the tombs, crying out and cutting himself with stones (Mark 5:5).

A Darkness That Can Be Felt

Whole cities, regions, states, and nations can be dominated by a thick covering of darkness. "A darkness that can be felt" is a correct biblical description of darkness that persists over many and most cities:

Now when Jesus heard that John had been put in prison, He departed to Galilee. And leaving Nazareth, He came and dwelt in Capernaum, which is by the sea, in the regions of Zebulun and Naphtali, that it might be fulfilled which was spoken by Isaiah the prophet, saying: "The land of Zebulun and the land of Naphtali, by the way of the sea, beyond the Jordan, Galilee of the Gentiles: The people who sat in darkness have seen a great light, and upon those who sat in the region and shadow of death light has dawned. From that time Jesus began to preach and to say, 'Repent, for the kingdom of heaven is at hand'" (Matt. 4:12-17).

Notice that the darkness affected the people to the point that they sat in darkness, resting, enjoying the darkness. The darkness was upon a region, a geographical darkness, in the land of Zebulun and Naphtali. A seat of Satan is a geographic location that is highly oppressed and demonically controlled by a certain dark principality. From this demonic seat the enemy conducts warfare on the city, region, state, or nation. To penetrate the regions of darkness, we must discern where the seats of Satan exist and how to successfully destroy them spiritually. We must discern our Zebulun and Naphtali.

Each Region Is Unique in Darkness

Each region has its unique historical, cultural differences and spiritual destiny (Matt. 4:15, 16; Acts 17:5, 9; 18:9, 10).

Each region has its own unique level of darkness (Exod. 10:21; Isa. 60:2). When you compare the levels of darkness in certain cities to others, it is very obvious that some have thick, deep-felt, controlling darkness while others have weak darkness, easily penetrated. Every region must be spiritually discerned and then strategized.

Each region has people darkness unique at that time to that region. In 1980 a news broadcaster presented a segment about residents living in the Loveland area of New York State who exhibited an unusually high frequency of cancer and leukemia. An investigative search revealed a toxic waste leakage that flowed into the residential water tables, infecting hundreds of families. These unsuspecting people were living right on top of life-threatening chemicals, but were unaware that these unseen toxins were slowly seeping into their bodies. Darkness upon a region will have a deep impact upon the people who sit under it for years, decades, and generations. Violence, immorality, occult and many other forms of spiritism, witchcraft, and New Age will seep into the water tables and slowly destroy every area of spiritual and domestic life (Ps. 143:3; Prov. 2:13; 4:19; Isa. 42:7; John 3:19).

Desensitized by Darkness

The spiritual covering of darkness over a region will slowly transform the people of that region. When a city culture is given over to evil powers and evil practices, the door for demonization is opened and people may be influenced by or ignorantly welcoming evil spirits into their lives. Luke 22:3 states that Satan entered into Judas Iscariot, and Acts 5:3 states that Satan filled the heart of Ananias, causing him to lie to the Holy Spirit and to withhold part of the money he and his wife Sapphira made when they sold a piece of property. In both cases, evil had profound influence upon the human heart, mind, will, and emotions.

People who live under a thick covering of darkness may well be candidates for Satan to fill their lives with his power to do evil. Today's culture sits under individualism and secularism, and relativistic values envelope people and condition their minds and spirits. An increased exposure to immorality and vulgarity desensitizes people and leads to a diminished ability to discern good from evil.

This world's darkness of covetousness, ambition, lust, intellectual pride, sensuality, materialism, and worldly prestige makes for a darkness that can be felt and a darkness that must be penetrated. The apostle Paul described this doctrine of darkness as this present evil age (Gal. 1:4), the prince of the power of the air (Eph. 2:2) and those who walk according to this world (Col. 1:13).

Darkness Versus Light

This present evil age of darkness is contrasted to the age of light and righteousness in which Christ reigns above all evil rule, authority and power of dominion. These two powers, darkness and light, stand in direct opposition with strong conflict. One is a kingdom of sin and death in which demonic powers seek to influence, rule and torment people's lives. The other is the kingdom of life and righteousness in which Christ is Lord, bringing freedom and destiny to people's lives.

Paul states in 2 Corinthians 5:17, "Therefore, if anyone is in Christ, he is a new creation; old things have passed away; behold, all things have become new" and in Colossians 1:13, "He has delivered us from the power of darkness and conveyed us into the kingdom of the Son of His love." (Also Eph. 1:20, 21.) God has given us the power to penetrate this darkness over people's lives and the geographically dark areas where they live. Our mandate is "to open their eyes, in order to turn them from darkness to light, and from the power of Satan to God, that they may receive forgiveness of sins and an inheritance among those who are sanctified by faith in Me" (Acts 26:18).

Dismantling the Darkness with Spiritual Equipment

We, as the City Church, need the following spiritual equipment to successfully deal with the spiritual darkness over people, places, cities, and regions:

- We need spiritual perception and spiritual intelligence to see things undetected by natural eyes. We need spiritual discernment about people and geographical areas and insight to judge whether the source behind the power is human, satanic, or Holy Spirit generated.

- We need a biblical worldview which understands that there is both a spiritual realm and a material realm. Behind the visible is the invisible. Demonic forces may be very active in our Western society and yet totally undetected by the Western worldview. Though many Westerners retain a vague belief in God, most deny that other supernatural beings even exist. Indeed, unlike most of the peoples of the world, we Westerners divide the world into what we call the natural and the supernatural; then we largely disregard the supernatural. The Westerner's skepticism and scientific rationalism says that if something cannot be seen, measured, or proven through reason, it simply does not exist or, at the very least, should be doubted (Acts 6:12, 13).

- We need to establish strategic prayer centers in every city, in every church, and then in every Holy-Spirit-covered home that will open up a gate to heaven to break through the thick covering of evil and darkness (Gen. 28:15-17; John 1:5; 8:12). We must recognize and stand against the territorial spirits that lie behind the chronic historical problems in our cities. We do this through intercessory prayer, preaching the cross of Christ, and moving in the supernatural with power to deliver people (John 8:12).

- We need to believe in the power of the gospel to penetrate darkness in any and all cities, delivering people and places from evil influences. We need to believe that we, the City Church, can reach every person and bring every household in touch with the true power and love of a living God. We need to release the whole church to reach the whole city with the whole gospel (Rom. 2:19; Col. 1:13).

Paving a Power Path

For it is the God who commanded light to shine out of darkness, who has shone in our hearts to give the light of the knowledge of the glory of God in the face of Jesus Christ (2 Cor. 4:6).

But you are a chosen generation, a royal priesthood, a holy nation, His own special people, that you may proclaim the praises of Him who called you out of darkness into His marvelous light (1 Pet. 2:9).

The City Church will become the people of power. Everywhere we go, a power path will open up as we become humble servants dependent upon God to release His power through us. The New Testament clearly indicates that the power of God is meant to accompany the gospel and to find expression through the lives of those to whom and through whom the message comes. It is right to bring the supernatural into prominence and to raise Christians' expectations with regard to it. It is right to want to be a channel of divine power into people's lives at their point of need.

As a City Church, we must desire to see the evil chains of darkness broken off any and all people who come in contact with the power of God. Chains broken off:

- Those who are economically and morally poor.
- Those who have spiritually become captives of demonic powers, oppressed of the devil; those with physical infirmities.
- Those who are blinded spiritually by the god of this world.
- Those who are captives of witchcraft, any form of the occult, or any kind of religious deception.
- Those who are under a curse: from the ignorant or intentional use of witchcraft, other hoaxes or games, demonic curses, or people curses. Those who have become increasingly disoriented or confused, continuously emotionally drained or debilitated, or increasingly plagued by inordinate fears.

Come, let us pierce the darkness, let us declare war on the city strongholds!

Arise, shine; for your light has come! And

the glory of the LORD is risen upon you. For behold, the darkness shall cover the earth, and deep darkness the people; but the LORD will arise over you, and His glory will be seen upon you. The Gentiles shall come to your light, and kings to the brightness of your rising (Isa. 60:1-3).

Changing the Atmosphere

The city can become a place where the spiritual atmosphere changes dramatically, allowing a new surge of Holy Spirit activity. Atmosphere speaks of a pervading or surrounding influence or spirit, a general mood or environment. In 2 Chronicles 5:13, 14, the atmosphere of the Temple was changed by the prayer and unity of the priests, and "the house of the LORD, was filled with a cloud."

In Genesis 28:10-17, Jacob experienced an atmosphere change when God showed up. Jacob's response was "How awesome is this place! This is none other than the house of God, and this is the gate of heaven!" Our cities can be a gateway to the supernatural, a place where God abides and His power is actively released.

Twelve Atmosphere Goals

The following are 12 atmosphere goals to pursue:

1. An atmosphere of **Open Heavens**: No spiritual hindrances allowed—breakthrough.

   We all have seasons when we are pressed on every side, darkness abounds, and the heavens seem as brass. The same thing can happen to a church or city. And, as in the case of most individuals, churches and cities can also achieve breakthrough. The forces of darkness can be pushed back through prayer, worship, unity, and servanthood. Strongholds of poverty, sickness, crime, and violence can all be broken. And God can open the windows of Heaven and pour out hope, healing, and revival. In the book of Luke, Jesus sent disciples ahead of Him into every town. They healed the sick, announced the kingdom of God, and rebuked demons. Satan fell like lightening. They had open heavens. We can experience the same thing today. Let's open the heavens in our churches and cities to prepare for Jesus.

2. An atmosphere of **Unified Expectancy**: No "business as usual" services.

If you announced that Jesus was going to appear in bodily form at your next service, the atmosphere around your church would be a lot different. People would arrive early, ball games would be taped (or forgotten altogether), and lost loved ones would be physically dragged through the doors. No one would stay home because they felt under the weather. In fact, the prospect of a healing touch from Jesus would be added incentive to race to church. And yet, Jesus has already promised to be in our midst every time we come together. Let's live like it! Remember, He did very few miracles in His hometown (Matt. 13:58). God help us if we're guilty of a "hometown" attitude. Jesus Christ is the most exciting, inspiring, and power-filled personality in the universe. When He shows up, no one sleeps in the pews. Give the Holy Spirit some liberty during your next service; then get excited—Jesus is in the house!

3. An atmosphere of **Supernatural Surprises**: He's no common, ordinary God we serve.

Jesus' first miracle was that of creating 150 gallons of very fine wine. This was no ordinary wedding gift, and He's no ordinary God. He healed a centurion's servant whom He had never met, yet let a dear friend, Lazarus, rot in a tomb for four days before raising him. He rebuked religious leaders and violently threw people out of church, but forgave adulteresses. He even stored his tax payment in a fish's mouth. God is awesomely supernatural, but He's not ordinary. Who could guess that a struggling church in Toronto, Ontario, would touch churches worldwide through renewal? That a simple drama called "Eternity" would lead more than 30,000 people to salvation during its first 12 months? That pastors would come together to pound stakes into the ground and see crime rates plummet in their city? God has supernatural surprises in store for your church and your city—supernatural power that will heal, deliver, revive, and restore. Just realize that the way God releases His supernatural power will probably surprise you.

4. An atmosphere of **Everyone Can Receive**: No limitations allowed to be placed on anyone.

   Rahab was a prostitute, yet she's included as a champion of faith in Hebrews 11. Paul was vicious in his persecution of the Church, but he brought the gospel to the Gentiles. David committed murder and adultery; Mary Magdalene was filled with demons; Gideon was a coward. There is no limit to what God can do with a life. Jesus promised to give the Holy Spirit to everyone who asks—Holy Spirit power, faith, healing, vision, peace, boldness, energy, and life. There is no room for condemnation and unbelief in the kingdom of God, especially right now. If God puts no limitations on a person's life, neither should we.

5. An atmosphere of **People Are Important**: No person is undervalued here.

   Flowers come in all shapes and sizes, some soft

and delicate, others strong and thorny, yet each one has a unique fragrance and beauty. People are God's garden; they are His bouquet, and He loves variety. In fact, Revelation says that He's purchased them from every tribe, language, people, and nation (Rev. 5:9). People are our inheritance and valuing them is what the gospel is all about. No, there's not many wise, not many mighty, and very few noble. In fact, they come just like the rest of us—thorny, fragile, and in desperate need of sun, rain, and pruning. We just need to love and to recognize how beautiful each one becomes in the hands of the Master Gardener.

6. An atmosphere of **Victorious Living Is Possible**: No defeatist spirit; God is able to deliver anyone at any time.

   We've all quoted the verses, "If God is for us, who can be against us" (Rom. 8:31); "I can do all things through Christ"(Phil. 4:13), and Nothing, absolutely nothing, is impossible with God (Matt. 19:26). But we are entering a season in which the Church needs to be charged with the power of these truths so that fear doesn't stand a chance. We can look adversity in the eye and know that God is powerfully working every detail to our advantage. It's genuine faith. Confidence in a God who is for us. . . . Who spared not His own Son and will graciously give us all things. It's a lifestyle that's contagious. It gives hope to the hopeless, makes a way when there is no way, causes darkness to flee in terror, and releases the miraculous power of a God who knows no defeat.

7. An atmosphere of **Reaching Our City**: No "hold the fort" philosophy here; we attack and take no prisoners.

There are times of visitation for every city.

Jerusalem missed one of its times, causing Jesus to weep. Nineveh responded and received mercy and revival. There is also a time of visitation for our cities. God is zealous to break every demonic stronghold—pornography, crime, prejudice, poverty, New Age—and to release compassion and life. There is an anointing on the Church to reach cities. Denominational barriers are crumbling, prayer is on the rise, young people are touching their generation, and darkness is running for cover. Joshua and Caleb looked beyond the giants to a land flowing with milk and honey. Our cities are no more challenging than those Joshua and Caleb faced. Spiritual Amorites and Canaanites will flee before us as grasshoppers. God longs to touch our cities, and we're His partners. Just like Joshua and Caleb, we are well able to take the land.

8. An atmosphere of **Financial Blessing**: No excuses or apologies; God is good and He desires to bless and provide for His work.

Abraham, Joseph, David, Solomon, and Job—these were some of the earth's wealthiest people. Each one received his wealth from God. God is not afraid of riches. In fact, He is rich in every regard and the source of all true riches. Why then do we shy from riches? We're commanded to care for the poor, send missionaries, preach the gospel to the ends of the earth, and reach our cities for Christ. It all takes money—lots of it. God is good. He desires above all things that we prosper and be in health as our soul prospers (3 John 1:2). God is a giver and finds great delight in blessing His children. Let's receive it gratefully and then follow His example. The Bible says, "Give and it shall be given," "The generous soul will prosper," and

"He that gives to the poor lends to the Lord." This year take liberality to a new level and then receive the promised blessing.

9. An atmosphere of **Communion**: Where the voice of God is heard clearly.

His voice, though seldom discernible to the natural ear, is the most powerful sound there is. One word from Him and the most troubled heart is comforted, the most confused circumstances are made clear, and the most fragmented relationships are healed. These are exhilarating days for the Church. We are seeing a fresh outpouring of the Spirit, growing churches, an increase of the miraculous, power encounters, and healings. But what is affecting the lives of people the most is hearing Him. God is talking to His people. He is revealing His love one word at a time. Decade-long bondages are broken in a moment. Prayer is taking on an added dimension: listening. More can be said in silence than from the pulpit, because it is Jesus who is speaking. Remember the story of Mary and Martha? Martha busily set the table and prepared the meal. Mary seemingly ignored her responsibilities and sat idly with Jesus. Yet Jesus said Mary chose the better part (Luke 10:42). In our Western culture, where activity is king and where success is measured by the entries in the daytimer, let's not neglect the better part. Let's keep our ears ever tuned to His voice.

10. An atmosphere of **Faith**: No pessimism about the future; God is in control.

Books about the end of the world have been topping bestseller lists for years. The writers seem to forget that God is in control and that not even a sparrow falls to the ground without His knowledge. God has promised to feed and clothe us and to fulfill every word that proceeds from His mouth. We serve a good God and the future is in His hands. He's promised a glorious Church without spot or wrinkle. We're not there yet, but we will be. How about your life? Are there still promises to be fulfilled? Then go for them; God is with you. Doesn't He want our loved ones saved, our cities transformed, and the gospel preached to every nation? Absolutely! And He's not going to leave His work undone.

11. An atmosphere of **Vision**: Where people see the invisible and do the impossible.

What do you see when you look at your church? Is it filled with worldly teenagers, uncommitted fathers, budget shortfalls, and carpet that needs replacing? Or do you see as God sees: tear-filled altars, discarded crutches, healed families, ethnic diversity, and the shout of triumph. He sees lifelong bondages to alcohol, drugs or pornography shattered, bitterness washed away in forgiveness, and families restored. He sees our cities' red-light districts overrun with churches, the poor being fed, the prisons emptied, and Bibles in classrooms. God sees things the way they can be. He sees with the eyes of faith. We must do the same. Only then can we do the things God sees us doing.

12. An atmosphere of **Worship**: Where the river of God is released in fullness.

True worship comes from the heart. It can happen in the quietness of our personal devotions or while cruising on a six-lane interstate highway, but there is a dynamic that's released in corporate worship when musicians and voices abandon themselves totally to adore the Savior. It's called the river of God. It's a tangible sense of the Holy Spirit's presence where faith arises, hearts are refreshed, and the circumstances of our personal lives take on a new perspective. The river of God also impacts the heavenly realm. As God is enthroned on our praises, heaven rejoices, darkness is dispelled, and His kingdom rule is extended. Lord, let every area of our personal lives and corporate services be marked by the spirit of worship. We grant You permission to interrupt our programs and discard our agendas to release worship. And Lord, let Your river flow.

When these 12 atmosphere changes are in place, our cities will be loosed, the shackles of bondage will be broken and the rescued ones will be led out of the dark corridors of hell and into the kingdom of light.

Personal Application

1. Even Christians can become desensitized to the effects of evil around them. Take a moment

to evaluate the felt darkness in your city. Rather than looking at the city, ask the Lord for eyes to see *into* the soul of your city. What steps will you take to confront the darkness in your city?

2. Before we can penetrate the darkness in the city, we must allow the searchlight of the Holy Spirit to reveal areas of darkness in our own lives. Has covetousness, ambition, lust, intellectual pride, sensuality, materialism, or worldly prestige gripped you or desensitized you to the pain of others? If so, ask God to change your heart.

3. As you read through the 12 atmosphere goals, which ones do you most need to implement? Goals can only be achieved when those setting them make a commitment to take action. Will you list some steps you will take to change the atmosphere in your church?

NOTES

1.   *26 Translations of the Old Testament*, Genesis to Esther (Grand Rapids: Zondervan, 1985), p. 1.

2.   Frank E. Gaebelein, *Expositor's Bible Commentary, New International Version, Vol. 2* (Grand Rapids: Zondervan, 1992), p. 24, 25.

3.   William Wilson, *Old Testament Word Studies* (Grand Rapids: Kregel Publications, 1978), p. 108.

4.   W. E. Vine, *Vine's Expository Dictionary of New Testament Words* (Old Tappan, N.J.: Fleming H. Revell, 1966), p. 267.

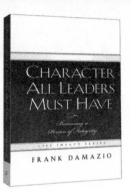

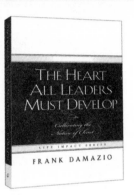
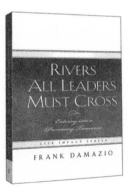

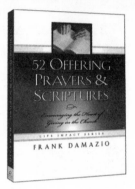

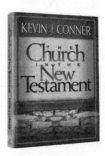

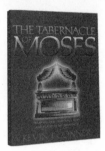
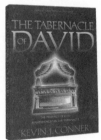